HOW TO SUCCEED
AS A
MASSAGE THERAPIST:

THE 3-SECRETS THAT EVERY
MASSAGE THERAPIST MUST
KNOW

Published by Haase Seminars Publishing

Printed in the United States of America
ISBN: 978-1522990895

Cover graphic used with permission from Adobe Stock Images
Author photo by Holly Ann Haase

2

"Always bear in mind that your own resolution to succeed is more important than any other."
– Abraham Lincoln

CHAPTER ONE

Defining Success

It is my hope that *all* massage therapists in the United States would be successful in their practices.

Every one of us.

There are numerous reasons as to why I dream of our mutual success, ranging from completely selfless to utterly selfish. On one hand, I hope we therapists can collectively make a difference in the lives of everyone we touch. My desire is that we can bring healing and relief to those suffering from pain and dysfunction, using our hands to help others become healthier.

On the other end of the spectrum, my desire for the success of all therapists is for completely selfish reasons. You see, if more of the population were to regularly incorporate massage into their lives, then there would be an increased demand for therapists and more massage therapists would have the funds to invest in my continuing education seminars!

When all therapists are busy and our appointment books are full, it is ultimately good for all of us.

The very definition of "*success*", however, is a bit different for everyone. What is "success" for you? Do you know what truly makes you happy? How can your business help you achieve that?

In Timothy Ferris' book, *The 4-Hour Workweek,* he talks about how most Americans work hard for their entire lives, saving money for retirement so they can eventually quit work and do the things they have always dreamed of. For some that might be traveling the world or volunteering to help build an orphanage in a third-world country.

Ferris suggests his readers consider living a simpler life instead, desiring less so they can live a "retired lifestyle" *before* their bodies start breaking down to the point they are unable to physically do what they have been daydreaming about for years. For me, his suggestion was spot-on. The idea of saving my entire life to "live retired" when my body is tired makes no sense. Instead, I have decided to live simpler so my money can go further, allowing me to do the things that make me happy now versus later.

The 4-Hour Workweek got me to thinking. What dreams am I chasing, or more accurately, whose dreams am I chasing? Who am I trying to impress and who am I trying to make happy? While some of my friends have built absurdly large homes and can brag about the pride of ownership, I would suggest that, perhaps, the 9,000sq. ft. home "owns" them. One of my high school friends was sitting with me by the lake on a summer evening back in 2013. As he fiddled with the beer in his hand, he was sharing about how life had slowly transitioned from joy to utter stress. He began listing off the things that were consuming his free time and then he paused. Slowly a look of disbelief began to form upon his face. He stammered as he formed his words. He said, "I was counting the other day and I realized that I have 56 combustion engines I have to maintain on my property. Cars, motorcycles, boats, snowmobiles, go-karts, lawnmowers, hedge-trimmers, 'weed eaters' … I don't own stuff, Bob… that 'stuff' *owns* me!"

Although his revelation reinforced my own decision to live simpler and live the "retired" life now versus later, something else happened that brought me absolute clarity.

Back in the spring of 2008, I was diagnosed with squamous cell carcinoma, a painful cancer in the base of my tongue. "No big deal", I thought. I would just follow the suggestion of my ENT and have it cut out. In the years that followed I ended up having 12-more surgeries. But in the fall of 2013 that slow-moving cancer suddenly changed and the recurring irregular cells morphed into a tumor that grew from what the surgeon described as the size of "half of a Tylenol® pill" to "the size of an Oreo® Cookie".

My team of surgeons were aggressively chasing an incredibly fast-growing cancer that was insidious and unrelenting. I was told that I would have to literally have the left-half of my tongue removed in order to save my life and I was sincerely frightened. If the surgeon erred, it was conceivable that I would never speak again.

My hemiglossectomy was performed on October 3rd, 2013 and my life changed forever. The least of the changes being I would never speak the same way again.

In January of 2014, following chemotherapy and radiation, I nearly died. Against the advice of my family and without knowledge of my medical team, I traveled to spend a few days at the Consumer Electronics Show (CES) in Las Vegas. I had wanted to go ever since I first saw the reports in the news every January since college.

Flying in a confined space and then spending time with 300,000 strangers from around the globe was admittedly a stupid idea considering I had white blood cell counts that had been obliterated from the chemotherapy. Shortly after returning I was found at home alone in bed under the sheets in complete rigor, my eyes rolled back, non-responsive to pain stimulus or light. After an emergency intubation that tore out my surgically modified throat tissues, the ICU concluded I had pneumonia, respiratory failure and systemic sepsis, any of which could have resulted in my death.

The good news is I fully recovered and am now cancer free. I learned to speak all over again, working daily on my diction, finding new ways to enunciate words so you can barely notice something is different.

It would be an understatement to describe this journey as truly life-transforming.

As I laid in the ICU with tubes down my throat and one piercing my belly that allowed direct nourishment, I had a lot of time to ponder and reflect. The experience of nearly dying allowed the superficial parts of my life to be peeled back. I was able to take a look at what was truly important and what was simply consuming my time. I had to dig deep and ask myself the very question I am asking you.

What makes *you* happy?

What is success to you? What does it look like? Is it storing up lots of cash for retirement? Is it changing the world in a specific, measurable way? Is it making an income that meets your needs while working less than 40-hours a week? Do you know? Can you articulate it?

I have heard it said *"The unaimed arrow never misses"*. Will you know success when you get there?

From a business standpoint, what does success look like? Do you want to be an employee your entire career? If your answer is yes, would your answer be the same if I were to tell you that you could literally make several times the income while working less hours? If you work for yourself, what do you envision your business to look like in 5-years? Will you work alone in a home-office? Perhaps success will be owning a large spa with 100-therapists? Perhaps a multi-disciplinary health clinic with a juice bar and health food store? Can you define it?

For the purposes of this book, we are going to define "success" as making a "livable income".

[To determine just how much you need to earn to charge and how many massages you need to give to be "successful", be sure to download our "Breakeven Analysis" from the Mastermind Diamond Circle Mentoring Group's "Materials" page at http://www.diamondcirclementoring.com.]

CHAPTER TWO

The 3-Legged Stool

In my 26 years in the massage profession, I have come to understand that being an exceptional massage therapist alone is not a guarantee of success for massage therapists. I have seen therapists with amazingly gifted skills ultimately fail at earning a living and I was saddened as I watched them give up a career they always dreamed of to go back to their previous and often unfulfilling occupations. It was through the observance of watching failures that I came to understand what ultimately is at the foundation for long-term success. A "three-legged stool".

As massage therapists, we need all three "legs" to not just be present, but be equally strong, each carrying its share of the load. Should any of the legs on a three-legged stool not be present, the stool fails at its purpose. For massage therapists, whether as an employee or for the self-employed, we must have:

> Leg #1: Exceptional skills as a massage therapist.
> Leg #2: Exceptional communication skills.
> Leg #3: Exceptional business and marketing knowledge.

Should the therapist find any of the three legs to be weak, or worse yet, non-existent, we may be able to balance our careers in the short term, but not for the long-term. All three legs must eventually be present and strong so we can have a career that truly flourishes and provides us with an abundance which enables us to live the life we choose and be a blessing to others in our world.

CHAPTER THREE

Massage & Bodywork Skills:
the First Leg

I remember when I was training in martial arts back in college. My best friend and roommate, Phil, was a 3rd degree black-belt in Takwondo and also my instructor. If you have ever seen an old Pink Panther movie with Peter Sellers as Inspector Clouseau, you probably remember his assistant, Cato Fong. Cato's mission was to surprise Clouseau at any time and attack him, keeping the inspector's fighting skills sharp. That relationship was a lot like my agreement with Phil. When least expected, he would throw a punch or kick and my job was to expect it and defend myself. Thankfully we didn't break every piece of furniture in our condo like Clouseau and Cato did in the movies.

During my 3-years of training, Phil taught me much more than just martial arts techniques, including a number of things that helped me later in my career as a massage therapist. He gave me practical advice, like when you break boards, never aim for the board. Instead, aim for what is behind the board and realize the board is simply a movable obstacle in your path. But more importantly, Phil taught me that I should not strive for the title of "black belt", but instead I should strive for technique. He said, *"Belts just show you are making progress. Besides, achieving the black belt only means you are finally at a place that you are ready to learn."* That is a lot like massage therapy.

Graduating from a massage school does not mean you are necessarily an amazing therapist. It does mean you have laid the foundation to learn. Even passing your licensing exam does not mean you have achieved "excellence", but it does show you likely know enough to not hurt your client.

To be exceptional in the field of massage requires a blend of several things. First, your *state of mind*, being "present", concentrating on your client's needs and "listening" to what your hands are palpating as well as focusing on your technique as you work rather than what you are going to make for dinner that night. Second, making every massage your best, and having the internal confidence *you* are the best massage therapist in the world to help *this* client at *this* moment in time and you are going to be used to make a difference in his or her life because of your educated touch. This thought process will affect the confidence and assurance that can be felt in your touch. Trust me, your clients feel it when you are unsure.

Be careful in the common temptation of having confidence in your hands based on unfounded beliefs in pseudo-science. I have encountered more than my fair share of therapists that because they *believe* something is happening in the body then their thoughts alone create truth. They do not think they need additional training because they can "will" the changes in the client's tissues, creating reality with the power of their mind. If you believe that, then please go down to your local cancer hospital and start curing patients right now. They really need you. However, if indeed thought alone does not create the changes, then your confidence needs to come from learning and utilizing solid techniques that consistently make a difference in your clients.

Continuing your education requires just that: continuing education courses. I will not make this suggestion out to be an advertisement for my courses, but I will suggest you get references from others who have taken a course you are considering. Make sure the course is built on a foundation of sound anatomy and physiology. Can the instructor explain why the techniques work? Are the results reproducible and consistent?

Most importantly, is the technique even within your scope of practice in your state? There was an inaccurate continuing education course being taught in our area back in 2000 where the instructor was teaching massage therapists how to adjust the spine. I tried to get the course shut down but I failed. The instructor claimed to be a naturopath and because he was from a state with no naturopathic licensing, he was simply because he said he was.

This ethically-challenged behavior is happening more than you would think. I had to "invite a continuing education group" to not return to my massage school because I caught the instructor showing students how to use a Q-Tip cotton swab to stretch the muscles of the eye *behind the eyeball!* That is not in the scope of practice for any massage therapist in any licensed state. As a therapist paying for a continuing education course, you will need to think for yourself and be aware of your state's laws and statutes.

If I hand you a scalpel I bought on Amazon.com and proceeded to teach you how to remove a "suspicious mole" on a client, should you? No. The bottom line is this: Just because someone teaches a technique in a class does not mean you can actually do it legally.

If I can give any advice to therapists on how to be a better massage therapist, it would be this: Learn to give exceptional massage with exceptional touch. Many of the courses that will distract you from doing just that will incorporate the use of mechanical tools, rocks, potions, instruments, etc. rather than teaching you to just touch better. Find a few massage therapists in your area who are renowned for their excellence and tell them you would like to pay them their hourly rate for feedback. Give the therapist a massage with the instruction you want continual commentary on what they like and don't like. Have them tell you and show you how to make the technique better. If you cannot afford to pay for a professional's time, then consider giving free massage to clients who are seasoned receivers of bodywork. Tell them the massage will be no charge but *only* if they give you ongoing feedback on what they like and don't like. Do not be shy or easily let your feelings or ego be bruised. Try different ways to contact with the tissue. Experiment with speed and depth. Experiment with table heights. Look at changes in lighting, music and other external distractors all the way down to your thought processes. Experiment and practice and you will transform from giving "good" or "great" massage to a place where you transform into giving extraordinary touch. As your client, I do not care how many years you have been a therapist or what school you went to. I give no regard to what color your hair is, what gender you are or who you voted for in the last presidential election. All I care about is how your hands affect me, and the same will be true of your current and future clientele. People do not spread the word after experiencing mediocrity, but they cannot stop talking about the amazing. Let us collectively work towards helping the public expect "amazing" from every therapist they encounter until amazing is the new normal.

CHAPTER FOUR

Communication:
the Second Leg

Communication is Key

In 1992 I received a massage from a woman who was brand-new to the massage profession. She had called me on the phone and said she had recently received her massage license and asked if I would be open to receiving a massage in exchange for my feedback. Free massage? I did not hesitate. For the purposes of this book, I will refer to her as Angela.

From the moment Angela put her hands on me... I can only describe what I experienced as transcendent. Not prior nor since have I experienced hands that were as gifted as hers. It was for me the "Holy Grail" of massage and I have yearned to experience that quality of touch ever since. Why not simply go back and get massage from her? Because Angela is no longer a massage therapist.

The sad part of Angela's story is although her hands were extraordinary, she had a difficult time communicating. She seldom was able to look me in the eyes, her voice was quiet and lacked confidence of any kind. Angela's gifts remained entirely in her quality of work and she could not communicate as you would expect from the average adult, let alone as you would expect from a professional in any field of work. Even though I sent numerous clients to Angela, she eventually returned to her previous job at Pizza Hut less than 6-months from the date she obtained her massage license. Angela leaned on the support of a one-legged stool and had set herself up for failure as a massage therapist.

While many therapists think they would finally be successful if they could just learn a few more massage techniques, they are ultimately misguided. You are better off being mediocre within your technique if you at least have moderate communication skills to go along with your ability to market yourself. The mediocrity of three legs always has an advantage over the existence of a single, excellent leg. You cannot make a living as an artist if you cannot sell your paintings.

When presenting my *Secrets of Deep Tissue*™ course, I usually ask those in attendance if any of them are "teachers". One or two may raise their hands, saying they teach at a local massage school, but in reality, every therapist in the massage profession should be a teacher. We should be "teaching" and educating every client and potential client. Unless you are providing relaxation massage and purposely limit communication so your client can relax, most therapists find themselves engaging in conversations that range in topics other than what they are "doing" to client during the session. Clients who understand what you are doing end up being more "compliant clients" and will stick to their treatment plans, making massage a priority.

Communication about your treatment is not just imperative during the session, but also before and after.

While I was preparing support materials for my Mastermind Diamond Circle Mentoring Group, many of the massage therapists told me that they felt awkward in certain areas of their communication with clients. It became clear their lack of knowing what to say often led to avoidance of talking about certain things altogether.

Whether you have access to a business mentor or not, you might find it helpful to sit down with a fellow massage therapist or friend and work through some of the scenarios that make you feel uncomfortable with your clients.

The most common areas that my mentoring group has needed help with in communicating include:

- ▶ Giving a 1-minute "elevator speech", explaining what it is you do
- ▶ Talking about the true benefits of massage therapy based on real-world, study-based evidence [See http://www6.miami.edu/touch-research/Abstracts.html for studies on massage therapy benefits]
- ▶ Clarifying what your client's needs are and then clearly explaining what type of treatment you will be providing. Any areas that might be uncomfortable for you or your client should be explained thoroughly and you should obtain permission to work on certain areas, if appropriate.
- ▶ Setting appointments for the first time
- ▶ Rescheduling a client after treatment before he or she leaves your office
- ▶ Handling "no-show" and habitually late clients

Bringing Our Issues to the Table

It is my experience that massage therapists bring their own issues to the massage session. For example, if the therapist does not like having their own abdomen touched, they in turn assume that "everyone" doesn't like to be touched there. This results in the therapist avoiding the area rather than educating, clarifying and proceeding with the treatment.

Let's say a client drops dead from a heart attack on the floor of your reception area. You follow your training and determine that chest compressions are indicated but hesitate because doing so would make you feel uncomfortable, thinking to yourself, *"Surely the client would feel uncomfortable having her chest exposed and have someone pressing on it, right?* So you withhold the treatment that would "increase the person's quality of life".

I know. That is an absurd analogy, but that is the point. If you have the tools and knowledge to help your clients but do not because you assume they would not be *comfortable* with it, it is much the same. With this in mind, it is important to consider *how* we ask a question or how we address the client's situation because it will have a significant impact on how the client feels about the subject.

For example, if your client is suffering from Thoracic Outlet Syndrome because tension in the Pectoralis Minor muscle is likely pinching her Brachial Plexus, you might say:

"Mrs. Smith, that tingling in your arm is possibly due to a muscle in your chest pressing down on a nerve bundle. If I can massage and then stretch that muscle, the Pectoralis Minor, I think we can get you the relief you are hoping for. I will keep your breasts covered and use your own hand to hold the sheet in place to make it easier for me to work on you. If the technique is uncomfortable or you want me to stop, you'll let me know?"

Regardless of what needs to be communicated, your role in how that communication is handled will have a direct impact on the success of your business and part of that communication also includes client education.

Creating Converts

Forgive the analogy, but building a massage practice is a lot like a preacher trying to build a congregation. The two are more alike than you may realize. I will save you the comparative list, but it comes down to this: If a preacher wants to increase the number of people who attend his church, he will need to either steal members of another preacher's flock or convert new members. The same applies to you.

Often advertising and promotion are merely an attempt

to lure clients away from other therapists. But, if the client leaves for another therapist that easily, they will ultimately leave you for a new therapist down the road as well. However, if you can "convert" people who have not been receiving massage therapy services previously, you will not only build a business but you will build it with clients who are loyal to you. That conversion process is built upon educating the public about why massage is so valuable, and why you are the right person to provide it. Which brings me to my "Pizza and Beer" story from my college days.

Pizza & Beer

The reason most grocery stores have a fairly stable business model is people have basic needs that must be met in order to stay alive including shelter, clothing, sanitation, and most importantly, food and water.

In general, most humans would not consider massage therapy as a requirement for their very survival which makes massage a "want" versus a "need". For this reason, people usually pay for massage therapy services with their "discretionary dollars", the same money they set aside for things like a night at the movies or a new flat-screen television. The question is, how do you get a potential client to spend his or her discretionary dollars on massage so you can make a livable wage?

Back in my college days, my buddies and I referred to that conundrum as the *"pizza and beer"* question. When I walked into my dorm room with a new CD player (not a small investment back in December of 1982) my buddy said, *"Dude! Do you realize how much pizza and beer you could have bought for that much money?!"*

The point is, if *what* you want to buy is *better* than pizza and beer, <u>*you buy it*</u>. When it is not better, you buy the pizza and beer.

How does THAT story relate to massage therapy? More than you think. People do not *have to have* massage to survive. Right? Unless they have been *led* to believe otherwise. It is up to you to get the message out to not only convince your potential clients they need massage, but that YOU are the best therapist for their particular needs. Advertising is not about saying "Hey, I'm here! Buy what I have for sale!" Advertising is about getting a message out, building desire, educating, and making a call-to-action. Nobody knew this better than Steve Jobs.

Steve Jobs had a difficult task ahead of him. He needed to convince the world they needed the iPod, a product category that was barely existent. And he did. Apple has sold over 300 million iPods since they were first introduced back in 2001. Even more astounding was how Starbucks convinced a nation who was used to paying $1.00 for a "bottomless" cup of coffee that they should pay two to three times the price for just *one* cup and *no* refills. It comes down to creating a superior product, educating the marketplace and building a desire for what you have to offer.

Which brings us to Leg #3 ...

CHAPTER FIVE

Business & Marketing Knowledge: *the Third Leg*

Whether you are fresh out of massage school or have been a therapist for decades, your success still requires the knowledge of how to build your brand and market yourself. Even if you have been getting along with what you currently know, increasing your understanding of business and marketing can make your success not only consistently possible but feasible with less stress and effort.

The need to understand business and marketing is equally important regardless of whether you are an employee or work for yourself.

Employees

Therapists who work for an employer often make the

assumption that they are just an employee, but there is so much more to it. As someone who has owned several businesses and has employed hundreds of people, I can tell you employees are either an asset or a liability.

As my daughters each reached the age of 16 and began to look for their first jobs, I sat them down and explained not only how to interview, but how to interview the business owner or manager. I told them they needed to walk in the door knowing they were an asset and the employer would be lucky to have them. Like I explained to them, employees reveal themselves during their interviews. If they start asking about how much time they get off, what benefits they get and how fast can they advance, then they are usually a liability. Someone who takes from the company and who makes it less efficient and less successful. However, if the candidate starts interviewing me, showing me they have researched the company, and ask questions about my company's philosophies and how we handle various cultural issues, it shows me they will likely be an asset to the company, making us more profitable which in turn allows me to bless them with better pay and benefits.

As a massage therapist working for someone else, not only should you be excellent in your skills and communication, you must also understand how businesses succeed so your place of employment can grow and you can benefit from that growth. As an employee, you are also building your career longevity by building your "brand". When a client comes to a business for a massage, they will ask for anybody available, but if you know how to build your brand and work on your technique and communication skills, that same client will instead insist on seeing you.

Self-Employed

Working for yourself does not have to be an intimidating proposition. I've heard therapists say they would rather have a job because it is "more secure", but that is just not the case. If you have ever lost a job or had your employer cut your hours or simply make your life miserable, you know employment is not necessarily easy.

From my first day as a licensed massage therapist, I made the decision to work for myself. I was able to set my own hours, rates, work location, techniques I specialized in and so much more. The benefits for me have been beyond incredible.

What I wished I had known in my early years was how to properly market myself. By all standards, I was very successful. But I spent a lot of time and a lot of money advertising when I could have greatly benefited from having a mentor.

Now, 26-years later, I am able to be a mentor to massage therapists of all experience levels all over the United States. The most important things we spend time on after getting their individual goals spelled out is defining themselves, knowing their niche and then learning how to actualize their objective.

Defining Yourself

Defining who you are, what you like and what you are good at are not always the same thing. I had a friend back in college who absolutely loved to sing. Out loud. Everywhere. The problem was she was tone deaf and I didn't have the heart to tell her. When she gave me a gift of a recording she had made where she had sung several pop-songs at the time, I finally had to share with her the bad news and suggest voice lessons. The point is, just because you like giving a certain type of bodywork does not necessarily mean you are as good as you would hope.

In the marketing profession we use "focus groups" to get feedback about products or services. We pay people for their time, or at the very least give them food and drink, and then spend considerable time interviewing them for honest, raw, no-feelings-spared opinions about their true thoughts. It is not always easy to hear the truth, but it makes businesses better when we get the opinions of those who are most likely going to utilize our services.

You will need to solicit the opinions from your actual target market. For example, if I asked, "Would you like to have a Porsche or a Tesla?" (currently the two highest-rated cars in terms of customer satisfaction on the market), your answer would most likely be "Yes". But if I asked, "Will you buy one of those cars?", your answer would more than likely be "No" unless you happen to have a spare $100,000 to spend on a car, give or take. You need to get input from your current clients as well as those who fit the description of your "ideal client" . Which brings us to your ideal "niche".

Defining Your Niche

In order to make sure you are marketing your business correctly, you need to know your niche (your "target market). It might sound silly, but it is imperative for employee massage therapists as well as the self-employed. Obviously, if I am preparing some snacks for an open house for my niche who are 19-year old athletes from the local community college, I probably would not serve them caviar and champagne. More like chips and energy drinks. So who is your niche?

When describing your niche, you need to consider age, gender, education, interests, health, location, occupation and more. Defining your niche will help you target market not just your advertising, but also your massage styles and supporting business aspects.

When you try to make everyone your target market or your niche, you end up with an unclear business model. It might seem like limiting yourself that specifically would hurt, but it actually helps. Being an expert in a certain area opens doors and gives you credibility rather than limiting your future.

I had a graduate of my medically-based massage school tell me she was not only going to make mothers her niche, but she was going to make her business name match so there was no mistaking that mothers were who her business served. While you might think that limiting yourself to such a defined group would limit your clientele, it actually does not. Whether you are marketing to mothers, college athletes, geriatric or other defined categories, all of those in your target market have friends and family who could benefit from your work.

Years ago, I specialized in working with athletes at one of my clinics. One of my athletes was so amazed by my work she referred me her grandmother with a bad hip, her sister who had a desk job that gave her neck issues, her niece who was a ballerina, her uncle who played golf... you get the idea. Just because you target one specific audience does not mean you will not have "collateral damage" which sends you additional clientele from other niches. When you market to everyone, however, you end up looking bland and like "just another massage therapist". Be special by specializing.

Marketing

Now that you know who your niche is, you will have an easier time making decisions about what your office should look like, where it is located, what your professional dress code might be, and how you will market to them.

Marketing to college kids in Geriatric Weekly would be a poor advertising medium, regardless of what kind of a deal they can get on the rates. Choosing your niche will help save yourself from missing the very target you are defining for yourself.

Marketing to your niche does not have to involve advertising in the traditional sense which will save you much of the very income you are trying to earn for yourself.

Getting an understanding of how to do that will take knowledge, so I recommend finding a successful mentor to learn from in your area. *

If you are unable to get the mentoring you need, I would invite you to join the Mastermind Diamond Circle Mentoring Group which is designed to help massage and bodywork professionals grow their clienteles and businesses. For more information go to http://www.diamondcirclementoring.com.

Conclusion

Regardless of where you are in your profession, there is hope for you. Take a moment to contemplate and reflect on your goals and desires and then take an inventory of your own strengths. Not just in your massage technique, but your communication skills and business/marketing acumen. Where you think you are not as strong as you should be, that is where you should focus.

I truly believe that every current therapist in the country would be busy with a waiting list if each of us worked on strengthening our "three-legged stools" and educating the public on what we do and why they need us. Better us than pizza and beer, right?

All the best to you in your career!

In Health,

Robert B. Haase, LMP
Haase Seminars
www.haaseseminars.com
www.diamondcirclementoring.com
www.haasemyotherapy.com

About the Author

Robert B. Haase, LMP, has over three decades of training and experience in business building and has both coached and mentored hundreds of business and health professionals into success. He received his Bachelors of Arts in Business and Marketing from Western Washington University and has been licensed as a mas-sage therapist in Washington State since 1991.

Robert has served as the Director of Marketing for the National Certification Board for Therapeutic Massage & Bodywork and has served on numerous boards in his community. He is the founder of the Bodymechanics School of Myotherapy & Massage in Olympia, Washington and currently travels the country presenting his seminars on business and bodywork topics.

Having lived through the irony of being a public speaker who lost the left half of his tongue to cancer in 2013, his story has been covered by numerous national news agencies and he is now known for his motivational and "encouragement" speaking. You can view USA Today's "Inspiration Nation" coverage, originally airing on Seattle's King5 News (NBC Affiliate) on YouTube at https://youtu.be/R1BoBzbSMM0 . Seattle's KOMO4 (ABC Affiliate) aired a follow-up story in 2015 which can be seen at https://youtu.be/bDcOVBRKd9w.

www.diamondcirclementoring.com